Leaving My Homeland

A Refugee's Journey from the Democratic Republic of the
Congo

Ellen Rodger

CRABTREE
Publishing Company
www.crabtreebooks.com

Crabtree Publishing Company
www.crabtreebooks.com

Author: Ellen Rodger

Editorial director: Kathy Middleton

Editors: Sarah Eason, Kelly Spence, and Janine Deschenes

Design: Simon Borrough, and Jessica Moon

Cover design: Jessica Moon

Photo research: Rachel Blount

Proofreader: Wendy Scavuzzo

Production coordinator and prepress technician: Ken Wright

Print coordinator: Margaret Amy Salter

Consultants: Hawa Sabriye and HaEun Kim,
Centre for Refugee Studies, York University

Publisher's Note: The story presented in this book
is a fictional account based on extensive research
of real-life accounts by refugees with the aim to reflect the
true experience of refugee children and their families.

Written and produced for Crabtree Publishing Company
by Calcium Creative

Photo Credits:
t=Top, bl=Bottom Left, br=Bottom Right

Dreamstime: Antonella865: p. 17t; Flickr: MONUSCO/Abel Kavanagh: p. 18b; Getty Images: George Pimentel/WireImage: p. 29c; Jessica Moon: pp. 3, 16b; Shutterstock: Antonella865: p. 17t; Valeriya Anufriyeva: p. 12, 23t; Artskvortsova: p. 16br; Boris15: p. 10c; Brothers Good: p. 8t; Sam Dcruz: pp. 5t, 14c, 18t, 20; Anca Dumitrache: p. 9t; Oleg Golovnev: p. 7t; H3x: p. 14t; Hadrian: p. 27; IKuvshinov: p. 12–13fg; Jane Kelly: p. 26bl; LOVE YOU: p. 5b; Mclek: p. 24–25; MSSA: pp. 15t, 21b, 29t; Oasisk: p. 8b; Gail Palethorpe: p. 26c; Pavalena: p. 21tr; Pimchawee: p. 19b; John Michael Evan Potter: p. 6; Jane Rix: p. 24; Route55: p. 10tr; Seita: pp. 14–15b, 22–23bg; Sentavio: p. 10l; Weredragon: p. 7b; What's My Name: pp. 13t, 26t; Xveron90x: p. 17b; Wikimedia Commons: SSgt. Jocelyn A. Guthrie: p. 22; MONUSCO/Sylvain Liechti: pp. 11t, 15c; Oasisk: p. 8b; Neil Palmer (CIAT) (www.flickr.com/people/ciat/): p. 16c; Ken Wiegand: p. 9b.

Cover: Shutterstock: Prazis (bottom); Jessica Stamp (right).

Library and Archives Canada Cataloguing in Publication

Rodger, Ellen, author
  A refugee's journey from the Democratic Republic of the Congo / Ellen Rodger.

(Leaving my homeland)
Includes index.
Issued in print and electronic formats.
ISBN 978-0-7787-3126-9 (hardcover).--ISBN 978-0-7787-3156-6 (softcover).--
ISBN 978-1-4271-1879-0 (HTML)

     1. Refugees--Congo (Democratic Republic)--Juvenile literature. 2.
Refugees--Canada--Juvenile literature. 3. Refugee children--Congo (Democratic
Republic)--Juvenile literature. 4. Refugee children--Canada--Juvenile literature.
5. Child soldiers--Congo (Democratic Republic)--Juvenile literature. 6. Refugees-
-Social conditions--Juvenile literature. 7. Congo (Democratic Republic)--Social
conditions--Juvenile literature. I. Title.

HV640.5.A3R63 2017   j305.9'069140967510971   C2016-907089-1
                                                     C2016-907090-5

Library of Congress Cataloging-in-Publication Data

Names: Rodger, Ellen, author.
Title: A refugee's journey from the Democratic Republic of the Congo /
  written by Ellen Rodger.
Description: New York, N.Y. : Crabtree Publishing, 2017. |
  Series: Leaving my homeland | Includes index.
Identifiers: LCCN 2016054842 (print) | LCCN 2016059684 (ebook) |
  ISBN 9780778731269 (reinforced library binding : alk. paper) |
  ISBN 9780778731566 (pbk. : alk. paper) |
  ISBN 9781427118790 (Electronic HTML)
Subjects: LCSH: Refugees--Congo (Democratic Republic)--Juvenile literature. |
  Refugees--Canada--Juvenile literature. | Refugee children--Congo
  (Democratic Republic)--Juvenile literature. | Refugee children--Canada--
  Juvenile literature. | Child soldiers--Congo (Democratic Republic)--Juvenile
  literature. | Refugees--Social conditions--Juvenile literature. | Congo
  (Democratic Republic)--Social conditions--Juvenile literature.
Classification: LCC HV640.5.Z28 R64 2017 (print) | LCC HV640.5.Z28 (ebook) |
  DDC 362.7/7914096751--dc23
LC record available at https://lccn.loc.gov/2016054842

Crabtree Publishing Company
www.crabtreebooks.com   1-800-387-7650

Printed in Canada/022017/CH20161214

Published in Canada
Crabtree Publishing
616 Welland Ave.
St. Catharines, ON
L2M 5V6

Published in the United States
Crabtree Publishing
PMB 59051
350 Fifth Avenue, 59th Floor
New York, New York 10118

Published in the United Kingdom
Crabtree Publishing
Maritime House
Basin Road North, Hove
BN41 1WR

Published in Australia
Crabtree Publishing
3 Charles Street
Coburg North
VIC, 3058

What Is in This Book?

Leaving the Democratic Republic of the Congo

For many years, there has been conflict and **civil war** in the Democratic Republic of the Congo (DRC). This has made the country a very **unstable** and dangerous place to live. People are frightened because armed **militias** roam the countryside, fighting the government army. The militias want to gain control of the country and its valuable **natural resources**. These groups kill families and force children as young as six years old to join them as soldiers.

The DRC is in Central Africa. It is the second-largest country in Africa. It has a population of more than 77 million.

Central African Republic

South Sudan

Cameroon

Republic of the Congo

Gabon

Democratic Republic of the Congo

Uganda

Rwanda

Burundi

Tanzania

Kinshasa

Angola

Lubumbashi

Zambia

Atlantic Ocean

The endless violence forces people to flee their homes. People who leave their homes but remain within the DRC are **internally displaced persons (IDPs)**. Others flee and become **refugees** in other countries. **Immigrants** leave their **homeland** to look for opportunities in other places. But refugees leave to escape danger.

More than 40 percent of people in the DRC are under the age of 14. Many child refugees have fled the DRC. They now live in refugee camps in neighboring countries.

UN Rights of the Child

Every child has **rights**. Rights are privileges and freedoms that are protected by law. You have the right to special protection and help if you are a refugee. The United Nations (UN) Convention on the Rights of the Child is a document that lists the rights of children all over the world. Think about these rights as you read this book.

My Homeland, the DRC

Hundreds of years ago, several powerful African kingdoms ruled the land now known as the DRC. These kingdoms were centers of **trade**, where arts, crafts, and music thrived for hundreds of years. By the 1800s, some of these kingdoms had made contact with European explorers and traders. The Europeans believed they had the right to control the land and the Native peoples living there. Many Africans were captured by traders who sold them as slaves.

Many African kingdoms traded ivory, from the tusks of elephants, with European settlers.

In the 1860s, King Leopold II of Belgium wanted more wealth and power. He knew he could become rich by setting up a **colony** and selling its natural resources. Leopold started a private colony in Africa that only he controlled. He called this colony the Congo Free State.

Leopold made millions of dollars by forcing the people of the Congo to work on his **rubber plantations**. After stories of Leopold's brutal rule leaked out, people around the world wanted him to give up control of the Congo. The Belgian government paid Leopold millions of dollars for the colony, and took it over in 1908. It was then renamed the Belgian Congo.

King Leopold (right) was a cruel ruler. He had his plantation workers' hands cut off if they did not make enough rubber. Plantation workers were often killed for not producing enough rubber.

In 1960, the country became **independent**. It was then renamed the Republic of Congo. However, the new country was unstable. For the next 50 years, it had many leaders and experienced **ethnic conflict**. A civil war took place, along with mass killings and **rebellions**. Millions of people were killed.

The DRC flag has changed many times over the years. The current flag was adopted in 2006.

DRC's Story in Numbers

There are more than

200

ethnic groups in the DRC.

Etienne's Story: My Life Before the Conflict

I was born in a small village. My mother's family had lived there for many years. We later moved to Lubumbashi, which is a beautiful city. It is a mining center and is the second-largest city in the DRC. Only the capital Kinshasa is bigger.

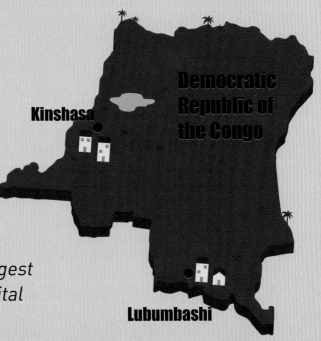

Democratic Republic of the Congo

Kinshasa

Lubumbashi

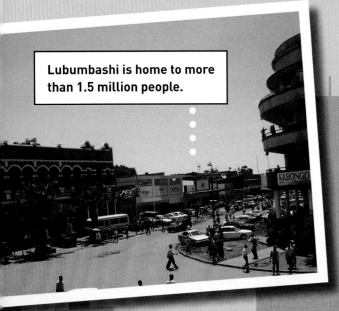

Lubumbashi is home to more than 1.5 million people.

In Lubumbashi, my father was a teacher. He had an important job at a good school. We had a good life. My father was an educated man. He wanted me, my older brother Claude, and my younger sister Martine to be educated, too. At school, we studied in French. However, at home we spoke our native language, Kingswana (Kiswahili).

We went to football (soccer) games. We also visited the zoo to see the lions and snakes. My favorite football team, TP Mazembe, plays in Lubumbashi. Sometimes, on Saturdays or special days, we had a party called a fete. We ate tasty foods, such as fufu, which is made with cassava. We also played games and had fun.

Even when things were bad in my country, and there was a lot of fighting, my life at home was happy.

Cassava is one of the most important crops grown in the DRC. Here, Congolese women dry cassava to make chips.

DRC's Story in Numbers

Lubumbashi is the mining capital of the DRC. More than

3 percent

of the world's **copper** comes from the DRC. More than half of the world's **cobalt** comes from the country.

A Violent History

When the Republic of Congo gained independence in 1960, a man named Patrice Lumumba became its president. But he was killed within months of coming to power. In 1965, Mobutu Sese Seko seized power. He was a **dictator** who stole the country's money, lived like a king, and refused to pay the army. In 1971, Mobutu changed the name of the country to Zaire.

Mobutu is shown here (top left) on this Zaire stamp. Zaire fell apart under his rule.

Militias from neighboring Rwanda and Uganda entered Zaire by force in 1997, leading to a civil war. The militias forced Mobutu out of power because they wanted access to the natural resources that could be mined in Zaire. The militia wanted to sell them to pay for armies and wars in Zaire and other African countries.

With Mobutu gone, Zaire became the Democratic Republic of the Congo. Another ruler named Laurent-Désiré Kabila made himself president, with the help of the Rwandan militia. At first, he supported the militia who had helped him gain power. However, he later kicked them out.

Kabila was killed in 2001. His son Joseph then took over. After six long years, the civil war ended in 2003. More than 5 million people died, and 2 million people became refugees. Even though the war has officially ended, militia groups still roam the countryside. They continue to fight to control the country, and its precious natural resources. They kidnap children and force them to become soldiers. It is believed that 30,000 children, aged six to eighteen, are soldiers in the DRC. Many are killed during fighting. Some escape, but it is not easy for them to return to the lives they had before.

Soldiers from other countries, called peacekeepers, have been helping protect the Congolese people from conflict since 1999.

UN Rights of the Child

You have the right to protection and freedom from war. Children under 15 cannot be forced to go into the army or take part in war.

Etienne's Story: We Leave Lubumbashi

My country has experienced many years of conflict. There is always fighting. My father had some political views that did not agree with those of the government. He got into some trouble when he spoke out against the government. He became worried about our family's safety, and thought we would be out of harm's way with my mother's family. He sent me, my mother, and my sister to live with my grandmother in her village. My older brother stayed with my father.

In many villages, aunts, uncles, and cousins live next door to each other. Maize, or corn, and other crops are grown in nearby fields.

the DRC's internally displaced persons

Living with host families: 72%

Living in informal camps: 28%

By 2013, there were

2.9 million

internally displaced persons in the DRC. Seventy-two percent were living with **host families**. Twenty-eight percent were living in **informal** camps.

By sending us away, my father thought he could keep us all safe. But nowhere is safe. The soldiers and militias come to many towns and villages.

I missed my father and brother. I did not know when I would see them again or when we could go home. But I liked the village. We had cousins there. We went to school, but it was not as good as my school in the city. I played football with my friends and cousins. I also worked in my grandmother's fields to help my family, growing food to eat and sell.

Surviving During Conflict

It is difficult to live in a country that has struggled with many years of conflict. People never feel completely safe. Millions of people in the DRC have been forced to leave their homes because of the violence. They sometimes go to places in their country that are safer, such as villages where there is no fighting. Or they may travel to refugee camps outside of the country.

Internally displaced persons and refugees walk long distances to safety. They leave with whatever they can carry.

Refugees from the DRC walk to safety. These children carry clean water in plastic jugs. No one knows where they will find water or food along the way.

To save their lives, IDPs and refugees leave behind their homes, jobs, schools, and everything they know. Often, families are separated. Sometimes, family members are lost along the way.

When people arrive at a safe place, they stay with family, friends, or anyone who will take them in. They may live for years in **temporary** housing, never feeling safe.

Life is no longer the same for internally displaced persons. Children might not go to school any more. Instead, they may have to work to help support their family.

If it seems safe to return, people may go back to their cities and villages. However, it can be many years before people feel it is safe enough to go home.

If they are lucky, refugees can take some possessions when they flee. Most just bring what they need to survive.

Etienne's Story: Kidnapped

Women tending fields are in danger of being kidnapped by militias.

I was working in my grandmother's fields when the soldiers came. They had guns and made me go with them. We walked for hours to a camp. I was confused and scared but I tried not to show it. At the camp, I became a soldier. I was taken by a militia group that wanted to get rid of the government. My commander said my family was dead and my fellow soldiers were my new family. I was eight years old.

There were many other boys and girls at the camp. The soldiers taught us to march, fight, and kill. We were forced to fire our guns at innocent people in villages. We were given drugs that numbed us against the terrible things we were forced to do. My commander said if we tried to escape, he would hunt us down.

Not everyone trusts government soldiers. Sometimes they recruit child soldiers, too.

He said if our families were alive they would not want us back because we were killers. Each day, I did what I had to do to survive.

I wanted to see my family again. Even if the village was burned to the ground, I knew my father and brother were in Lubumbashi. One day, we were sent to attack a village. I saw a chance. I ran off into the forest. I kept running and hiding for days.

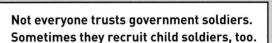

Child soldiers such as Etienne often have to survive on whatever food they can find.

Near a road, I heard trucks. I ran to them screaming "Take me home!" These soldiers were good. They brought me to a **nongovernmental organization** (NGO) that helped me. I was sent to a **reintegration** center in Bukavu. There, I felt safe. I was taught not to be a soldier. I could go to school and learn again. The teachers also helped me find my family.

Child Soldiers

Child soldiers are boys and girls under the age of 16 who are used in war or conflict. In the DRC, children as young as six serve in militias, rebel groups, and the country's army. Some are convinced to join by promises of money or protection. Others are kidnapped and forced to fight.

Violence and guilt are used to control child soldiers. Child soldiers are forced to kill villagers and other soldiers. They are sometimes even made to hurt their own families. They are also used to carry heavy loads of weapons or food. Some act as messengers, spies, or cooks.

The people who kidnap child soldiers believe children are easy to control.

International law allows people aged 16 and older to join the armed forces. People cannot fight in violent conflict until they are 18 years old.

Child soldiers are treated horribly. They may be beaten or killed if they do not follow orders. It is a dangerous, fear-filled life spent moving from camp to camp. They have little hope of escaping.

If they do manage to escape, child soldiers cannot just return to a normal life. Because they have been soldiers, they are considered dangerous. Some are put in detention, or jail.

Many child soldiers suffer from **trauma**. Some no longer have families, or their families and villages may be afraid of them because of their violent past. To help them, aid organizations such as the United Nations Children's Fund (UNICEF) have built reintegration centers in the DRC. These centers help child soldiers learn how to live without violence. The centers provide classes that help children learn new skills. They also teach boys and girls how to cope with their traumatic experiences.

DRC's Story in Numbers

15–30 percent
of new soldiers in the DRC army are under 18.

30,000
Congolese children have been child soldiers.

30–40 percent
of child soldiers are girls. An estimated

60 percent
of fighters in the eastern DRC are thought to be children.

Etienne's Story: The Refugee Camp

I was reunited with my mother and sister at the reintegration center in Bukavu. My country was still not safe, and we could not find my father and brother. My mother did not want me to be stolen again. We no longer had a home, and she was afraid of the violence in our country. We decided to leave. That is how we came to Burundi.

There are many wars and conflicts in Central Africa. As a result, refugee camps are overcrowded. People live in tents and often wash in nearby rivers.

Our camp was near the capital Bujumbara. It was very crowded and not always safe. But we could go to school there. I was happy to go to school because I had missed so much time. I promised myself I would be educated like my father. I knew he would want me to protect my mother and sister.

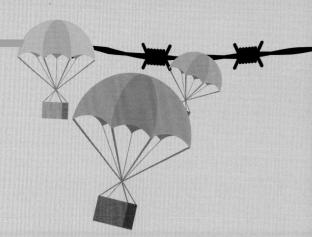

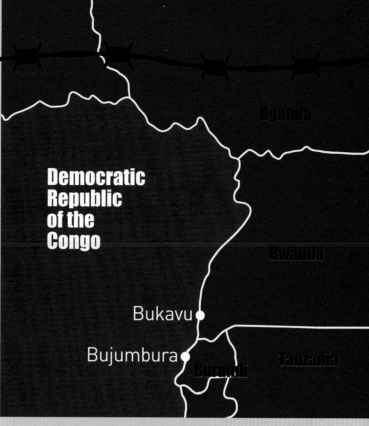

Democratic Republic of the Congo

Uganda

Rwanda

Bukavu

Bujumbura

Burundi

Tanzania

My sister was sick at the camp. The food was not good. The doctors there helped her, but my mother was very worried. She did not want my sister to die. She told the camp workers about her sister who lives in Montreal, Canada. We were very lucky to have a relative who lives across the ocean.

In the camp, we **registered** as refugees. Later, we applied to be refugees in Canada. There were many applications, and the process took a long time. We had to be interviewed, and we filled out many forms. We stayed in the camp for three years before we could go to Canada.

UN Rights of the Child

You have the right to the best health care possible, safe water to drink, nutritious food, a clean and safe environment, and information to help you stay well.

Where to Go?

Violence is the main reason people leave the DRC. Most DRC refugees seek **asylum** in neighboring Central African countries. While some African nations are safe, many of these countries are still unsafe and unstable. In fact, there are people who seek protection from violence in the northern DRC even though there is conflict there.

Soldiers of the Congolese Army struggle to maintain security within the DRC because of constant attacks by militias.

DRC refugees live in camps and **host communities** in Uganda, Rwanda, Tanzania, Burundi, Kenya, South Sudan, and other countries. Many of these refugees return home when it is safe. Refugees also seek asylum in France, Belgium, the United States, Canada, and other countries.

Survival would be difficult without aid organizations such as the International Rescue Committee and the United Nations High Commissioner for Refugees (UNHCR).

When refugees flee, they rely on people to help them along the way. This includes villagers who take in internally displaced persons, even though they are poor themselves. Aid organizations help set up camps and register refugees. They provide food, shelter, and medicine to refugees who have left their countries.

DRC's Story in Numbers

Since 2011,

42,454

DRC refugees have returned home from out-of-country camps.

245,052

DRC refugees live in camps in neighboring Rwanda.

Etienne's Story: My New Home in Canada

The day we left for Canada, my heart was full of joy. But I was also sad to be leaving my homeland. No one knew if my father and brother were still alive. It felt as though we were leaving them behind. We still do not know if they are alive.

It was my first time on an airplane. In the sky, I gazed down at my country, and saw the green forests and dark rivers. When we landed in Canada, everything was white and gray. I had never been so cold. My aunt met us at the airport and brought us warm coats and boots.

We live with my aunt in her small apartment in Montreal. She owns a restaurant and my mother works there. Many people in the city speak French. It helps to speak the same language.

To a refugee child, school buses and snow are strange and foreign. Snow appears only on the highest mountaintops in the DRC.

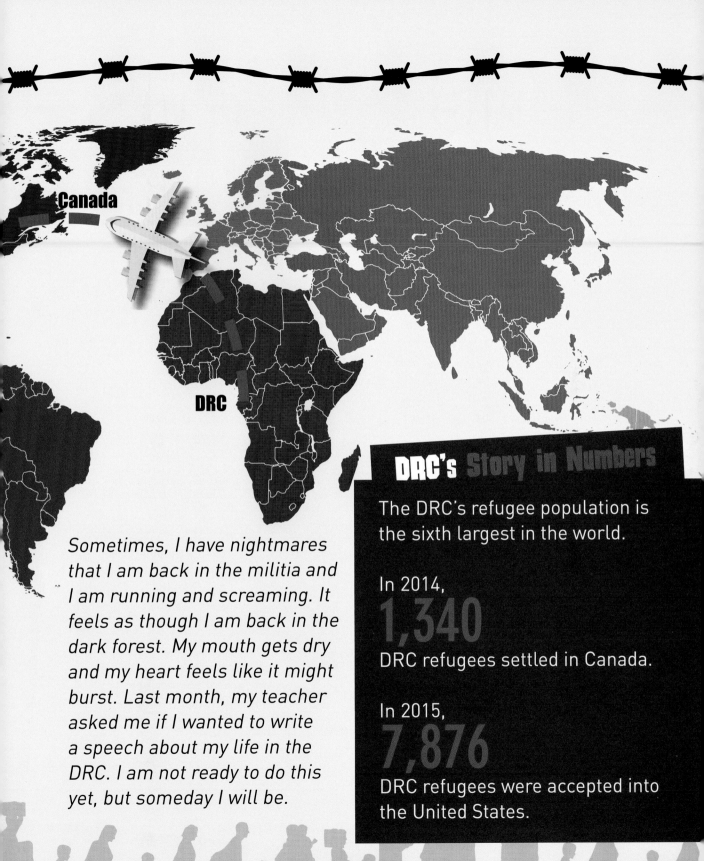

Canada

DRC

Sometimes, I have nightmares that I am back in the militia and I am running and screaming. It feels as though I am back in the dark forest. My mouth gets dry and my heart feels like it might burst. Last month, my teacher asked me if I wanted to write a speech about my life in the DRC. I am not ready to do this yet, but someday I will be.

DRC's Story in Numbers

The DRC's refugee population is the sixth largest in the world.

In 2014,
1,340
DRC refugees settled in Canada.

In 2015,
7,876
DRC refugees were accepted into the United States.

The Struggle Continues

Helping refugees requires short-term and long-term planning. In the short term, refugees need clean drinking water, food, and basic shelter such as tents. The long term means things beyond just survival. This may mean providing refugee children with schooling while they are in camps. It could also mean helping to resettle people in another country.

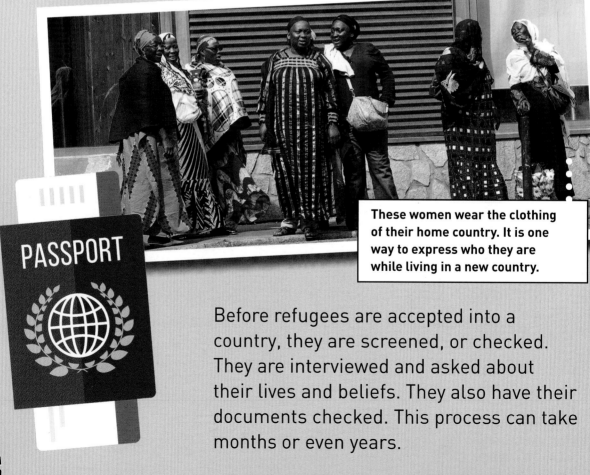

These women wear the clothing of their home country. It is one way to express who they are while living in a new country.

Before refugees are accepted into a country, they are screened, or checked. They are interviewed and asked about their lives and beliefs. They also have their documents checked. This process can take months or even years.

In some places, refugees are sponsored. This means people agree to financially support, or pay for, a refugee or refugee family for a certain amount of time. The government may also give refugees money until they can support themselves and their families.

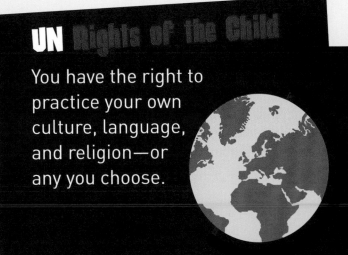

je suis un migrant

FRONTE

Congolese protestors in France urge the government to improve its policies on accepting refugees escaping conflict.

It is difficult to come to a new country and adjust to a new way of life. It is even more difficult for refugees who may be struggling with having lived through a war. They may fear the police or armed forces because of bad experiences in their homeland. Not everyone in their new country is friendly. Some refugees experience **discrimination**. Many Congolese refugees that arrive in North America may have to learn to read and write English. They may also have difficulty finding work to support themselves or their families.

You Can Help!

You can help refugees from the DRC and other countries, and make a difference for refugees living in your community. Here are some actions you can take to help refugees.

- ☑ Organize a bake sale or a used book sale at your school. Donate the money you earn to a charity that helps Congolese refugees.

- ☑ On February 12, celebrate Red Hand Day. This international event raises awareness about child soldiers in places such as the DRC.

- ☑ Volunteer your time at a local refugee or newcomer center. Many communities have these centers.

- ☑ Go to the library and learn about other countries. Use maps to find countries that have conflicts that create refugees.

- ☑ You can learn more about where refugees come from by reading books like this. You can also research refugees on the Internet with a parent or guardian.

- ☑ Learn the facts and speak out when you hear people saying discriminating things about refugees.

UN Rights of the Child

You have the right to help
from the government
if you are poor or in need.

HUMANITARIAN AID

**Michel Chikwanine (left) was a child
soldier in the DRC. He came to Canada
as a refugee. Today he is an author
and human rights speaker. He shares
his story to increase awareness about
the use of child soldiers in the DRC.**

Discussion Prompts

1. After reading this book, give
three examples of things you have
learned about refugees from the DRC.
2. What is the difference between a
refugee and an immigrant?
3. Brainstorm ways you can help a
refugee adjust to living in your country.

Glossary

asylum Protection given to refugees

civil war A war between groups of people in the same country

cobalt A metal that is mined and used in computers and batteries

colony A territory controlled by a distant country

copper A metal that is mined and used in electronic devices

dictator A ruler who has absolute power over a country

discrimination Unfair treatment, often based on race or religion

ethnic conflict Fighting that breaks out between groups, usually who have different religious or racial backgrounds

homeland The country where someone was born or grew up

host communities Groups of people or villages that offer to take in refugees

host families Families who let people in need live with them

independent Free from outside control

informal Unofficial

immigrants People who leave one country to live in another

internally displaced persons (IDPs) People who are forced from their homes during a conflict but who remain in the country

militias Military groups that are not part of a country's army

natural resources Materials from nature that are valuable

nongovernmental organization (NGO) A volunteer group that functions independently from a government

rebellions Acts of open resistance

refugees People who flee from their country because of violence or unsafe conditions

registered Was added to an official list

reintegration To bring back together

rights Privileges and freedoms

rubber plantations Large farms where rubber trees are grown

temporary Lasts a short time

trade Buying and selling goods and services

trauma The shock that follows a frightening event

unstable Often changing

Learning More

Books

Humphreys, Jessica Dee, and Michel Chikwanine. *Child Soldier*. Kids Can Press, 2015.

Prentzas, G. Scott. *Democratic Republic of the Congo*. Cherry Lake Publishing, 2012.

Williams, Mary. *Brothers in Hope: The Story of the Lost Boys of Sudan*. Lee and Low Books, 2005.

Websites

http://kids.britannica.com/comptons/article-9277871/Democratic-Republic-of-the-Congo
Learn all about the DRC's history and people in this comprehensive article by Encyclopedia Britannica.

www.playagainstallodds.ca
Play Against All Odds, an interactive game provided by the UNHCR, takes a player through the experience of a refugee.

www.redhandday.org/index.php?id=4&L=0
Learn about Red Hand Day, an international event that raises awareness about child soldiers all over the world.

www.unicef.ca/sites/default/files/legacy/imce_uploads/images/advocacy/co/crc_poster_en.pdf
Explore the United Nations Convention on the Rights of the Child.

Index

About the Author

Ellen Rodger is a descendant of refugees who fled persecution and famine. She has written and edited many books for children and adults on subjects as varied as potatoes, social justice, war, and lice and fleas.